How to Rank in Google

Google

SEO strategies post Panda and Penguin

JAMES GREEN

ISBN: 1484171403
ISBN-13: 978-1484171400

DEDICATION

This book is dedicated to Debbie, Amy, James and Boo.

CONTENTS

COPYRIGHT

ABOUT THE AUTHOR

Hi, I'm James Green and I've been an internet marketer for over 7 years now. I'm a simple family guy, with a lovely wife, 2 great kids and a cat called Boo!

I began doing internet marketing as a hobby to begin with and as a way to supplement my income.

I guess it took me around 2 years of making mistakes (and boy, I've made them all!) before I finally latched on to an area that I liked and that began earning me a reasonable income. I must have subscribed to just about every internet marketing course in that time and bought every book that was I thought was even remotely relevant to the industry I was in.

My initial mistakes mainly consisted of a combination of:

1. doing too many different projects at once ('rainbow-chasing', as I call it), and
2. doing all the projects badly!

I would fly from one scheme to another, trying to grab every opportunity and never quite seeing any of them through to the end.

However, I finally latched onto an affiliate marketing course which genuinely started working for me. I also learned the importance of concentrating on one project at a time!

After a few months of sweat things suddenly began to happen. I had produced what I thought was a fairly decent site, which started to rank quite decently in the Google search results and, lo and behold, the money started to roll in.

It really is a great feeling to start realizing an income for your efforts. In my case my website was earning me a passive income – one which continued to earn me money even while I was sleeping! At last, an income which would supplement by regular wages, I thought – I can start to pay off some of the money I had spent on all those courses and books!

It was slow at first, but using many of the techniques I had learned over the previous years, I was able to climb slowly but surely up the rankings. I wasn't a millionaire by any means but I was doing pretty good. My sites were getting recognized, I was getting REAL comments and even offers for guest posts along with a very healthy number of daily visitors.

Through time my ranking increased along with my bank balance, peaking at around 500 visitors per day on some sites. Not bad for a relative newbie, I thought.

Then I woke up one day to check on my site and BOOM! Google Panda had struck. My rankings virtually disappeared overnight. I was devastated. All that work for nothing! I thought at first that maybe it was a glitch. But no, my site had dropped from the hundreds to around 50 and there it stubbornly remained.

After cursing the evils of Google and feeling very sorry for myself, I decided to do some research to find out why my site had suffered so badly. It was then that a few home truths hit home:

I realized my site wasn't all that; it wasn't really giving people everything they wanted; it had a pretty high 'link-to-content' ratio and in spite of my previously high hits, my bounce rate was pretty high too (i.e. the average amount of time people were spending on the site was low). The great majority of users got to my site and simply left again. Looking back, I'm even surprised I did as well as I did!

I had religiously followed what is now outdated dogma: I had built each page of my website around specific targeted keywords rather than creating a site around a topic (more on this later) and a good user experience.

So I stopped feeling sorry for myself, took a step back and started over. From scratch.

I found out what worked and what didn't and copied the people who were doing well. I quizzed many seasoned internet marketers and SEO advisers. And tiny-step by tiny-step I developed a laser-targeted plan over the next year, testing each method as I went and measuring the results. I began to simplify, to break everything down into smaller chunks, throwing out the bad and keeping the good. I found out what Google liked and how to best deliver it.

But more than this, I became less Google-focused, and more user-focused. I also became less reliant on Google alone, which I think is key to your success.

As part of this plan I also addressed my time management and organization skills (which were badly in need of sharpening). With internet marketing, there are so many things in your head, so many things to learn and so many different strategies, it can become a little overwhelming. If you're not careful you can very easily end up flitting from one idea to the next like a honeybee, desperately hopping from flower to flower, gathering nothing but exhaustion.

It took a while to find that winning Blueprint, but I can honestly say that it was worth it. I'm happy to report that I recovered from both Panda, Penguin and all subsequent updates.

Mine's a happy ending and I'm confident that with the solid foundations I build, I will continue to be successful, regardless of whatever Google decides to do next.

And this book is my way of giving back, to share with you all that I've learned.

It's been a labor of love and I firmly believe that by following my strategies yours will be a happy ending too and that you too will enjoy a very healthy income from your sites for many years to come.

Here's to you and your own success!

James Green

1. WHO SHOULD READ THIS BOOK?

In a sentence, this book is for anyone who has, or plans to develop, a website that can make them a generous income. This may be in the form of an active income (e.g. providing a service or product) or as passive income (e.g. advertising or affiliate marketing).

If any of the following rings true, then this book is for you:

• if you've been hit by the Google updates, have been banging your head against a brick wall and just can't see how to recover;
• if you need more financial security or are just tired of your job and want to earn a decent income through your website;
• if you're stuck in a rut with your website, lacking focus and need guidance;
• if you've been procrastinating or suffering from information overload (very common);
• if you've tried countless SEO strategies, but your rankings remain stubbornly where they are;
• if you've started your website project itching with enthusiasm, only for it to flounder after a few months of not seeing any results.

Whether you're a hobbyist, a small business or an affiliate marketer, I'll reveal to you some extremely powerful (and sometimes surprising) new strategies that will help you rank and get that all-important trust from Google.

The internet is an amazing opportunity but so few people are using it to its full advantage.

In my view, there are 2 elements to having a successful website:

1.   Getting a decent number of hits every day, and
2.   Leveraging those hits.

If your goal is to get 1,000 visitors per day from your website, but you're not interested in making any money from it, then this book probably isn't for you!

After all, what is a website but a shop window? And if you're leveraging your site in the correct way and converting your visitors into customers, you won't need thousands, or even hundreds of visitors per day to earn a very comfortable monthly income.

But it's not just about the Google website rankings. I'll also show you how other sites can also bring in traffic and earn you money. Not only that, but I'll also show you how you can use other sites to your advantage, that will feed into each other in a very powerful way, constantly driving your site upwards and reinforcing that all-important trust.

I'll be keeping it light, concise and jargon-free, with as little waffle as I can get away with. But I'll also make sure that it's jam-packed with valuable content.

And watch out for…
Throughout this book I'll be highlighting certain sections with **Panda/Penguin Alert** – this will flag up new rules post Panda and Penguin to watch out for, so pay careful attention to these.

I also want to show you how you can not only compete with the big boys but can blow them out of the water with this blueprint, and for very little cost. Many of the tools and services I'll be mentioning in this book are free (or almost free) and unless you want to start using paid advertising, or outsourcing everything you do, to begin with you simply need a hosting account and a Domain name.

I'm assuming that since you're interested in how to rank well in Google that you already have a Website or at least know how to set one up, so I won't be patronizing you by talking you through installing WordPress, etc.

So turn off that TV, clear away all your clutter and make a commitment today to get that website off the ground and ranking, giving you the income you deserve!

Remember, a journey of a thousand miles begins with a single step!

2. ASSUMPTIONS

I want to keep this book tight, to the point, and relevant to my readers, with lots of easy to digest tips and tricks.

This book will be furnishing you with many little-known and extremely powerful strategies to propel your site beyond just about every competitor, on a minimum budget.

So in order to provide as much value as possible I don't want to fill it with lots of fluff about how to write a website or how to get a hosting account or a domain or how to sign up for a Twitter account. I am assuming that since you're here, that you already have a website and know the basics.

With this in mind, I'm assuming you know how to:

- Set up a hosting account (I use Hostgator, but you may not);
- Register a Domain name (although I will be including a section on how to select good Domain names);
- Create a website (or know someone who does!);
- Are reasonably technically competent (or know someone who is!)

In short, I'm assuming you've already been some way down the road of creating your own website(s), but simply need a roadmap for making it/them more of a success, particularly post Panda and Penguin.

So if you're still with me, then let's get started!

3. INTRODUCTION

On February 23rd, 2011, war broke out between Google and their enemy, the link farms. Google Panda was released, perhaps the greatest single change to their algorithms to date, dramatically affecting the way they ranked web pages, or more specifically, entire web sites.

Up until then, it was relatively easy for any reasonably internet-savvy company or individual to rank pretty well for a variety of keywords using tried and tested techniques, pretty much regardless of the quality of their content.

Once ranking, they simply littered the pages with either AdSense links or links to other fee-earning pages, usually in the form of affiliate links. And they enjoyed a steady and very healthy income stream from it too.

Google rightly viewed these 'ad-heavy' websites with disdain, which were often ranking at the expense of high quality sites, and they were keen to find a way to take them out of the game.

And in this major update they made a pretty good job of doing just that. Virtually overnight, it's estimated that around 12% of websites simply tumbled down the rankings and out of sight.

What did they do? Their new algorithm compared many low quality 'scraper sites' (those simply existing to redirect people to other sites, earning the webmaster a very nice income along the way) with known high quality sites and looked for key crucial differences between them. It concentrated on such things as over-repetition of keywords (known as 'keyword-stuffing'), duplicate content, and a high link-to-content ratio – a sure sign of low quality.

And when they found the culprits, they didn't simply penalize individual pages as they did previously, but shot down the entire site. This was a new way of thinking by Google and has completely changed the internet landscape ever since.

Following this update, the newsgroups were awash with complaints about Google's underhand tactics. But there was little sympathy among the SEO community as the vast majority of the complainers had been gaming the system for years, offering low-quality, spammy sites that offered little value to users.

However, it also caused many other casualties along the way. Many article directories simply fell out of the sky, virtually overnight. But more importantly (from my perspective anyway) it was affecting individuals who were trying to make a passive income from the internet. People like me. I was an affiliate marketer offering what I thought was a valuable service and producing fairly good content. Or so I believed.

But in the cold light of day, I had to ask myself a difficult question: was what I was doing really that valuable? Was I really offering the public what they really wanted? Was I going the extra mile for them and responding to their wants and needs? Was I joining in the conversation and really contributing to the party? The painful truth was that I wasn't.

Since then Google have released many subsequent updates to their algorithms.

Many websites had survived previous updates only to face a new nightmare: Google Penguin, which became self-aware on April 24, 2012. Their mission: to seek out and destroy websites that provided a 'poor user experience'.

But this book isn't about dwelling on the past, nor on cursing the search engines for the position we're in. And I promise not to waste good electronic ink on in-depth charts and tables, analyzing the various impacts of Google's latest algorithms. I also won't pretend to be able to second-guess what Google's next move will be either.

We all know in our hearts that what Google really wants is quality. And they aren't doing this for altruistic reasons – the more relevant the results they can deliver to the public, the more money they make. Simple. Their raison d'etre is to deliver the best results based on what they perceive the user wants. And they're pretty good at it too; and getting better all the time.

But they're also far from perfect, (don't even get me started on their, what can now only be described as, blatant disguising of their AdWords results in with the natural search results), and nor are their algorithms. You only need to do some searches to see that there are still some far from savory characters still making it onto page one of the results. But their algorithms are being updated all the time and I firmly believe that they will eventually weed these 'spammy' sites out, which can only be a good thing for the likes of us, I hope you'll agree.

"Well that's all very well", you say, "but why aren't they finding MY high quality website? I have good content and yet Google still continues to penalize me!"

You may very well have what you think is a worthy site, providing plenty of value but if it isn't relevant to the search terms you have chosen, and if you don't cover all the bases correctly, then Google (and all other search engines for that matter) are simply going to pick up their ball and go home (I'll be discussing this issue of relevance and quality in the next chapter).

Consider this – does your site fit all of the following criteria:

- Does it present a full, rich and interesting experience to your readers?
- Is your chosen subject something that many people actually want?
- Are all your articles 'on-topic' i.e. completely relevant to your core business?
- Does your niche have the right-sized audience? If your niche is too small, you'll struggle to achieve any decent search results; if it's too broad, the competition may just be too great.
- Are you interested in the subject you are talking about? If you're not, there's less chance that you will be bothered to keep your site maintained and promoted.
- Does your site have a coherent, easy to follow structure? If it doesn't users may have a confusing experience navigating around your site.
- Is there plenty of scope for related and relevant content e.g. articles, videos, books, interviews, etc. on your subject?
- Have you created a 'buzz' around your site, with lots of social interaction?

- Is your site completely current and up-to-date, with plenty of fresh content?

If all the answers to the above are "Yes! Absolutely!", then great, carry on! But if not, you may need to do a little soul-searching and consider whether you have chosen the right niche or are developing it in the right direction. Often all that is needed is simply a little tweaking to make it either more inclusive, or even more exclusive.

But just sit down and be honest at this point and make a list of areas where your site may be falling short before moving on.

Now there are even more rules and strategies to follow than ever before. They're also quite different post Panda and Penguin and many of the old ways no longer apply.

By following the steps laid out in this book, you will once again enjoy healthy rankings that will last many years to come. Not only that, but you will have Google as well as your many followers eating out of the palm of your hand.

And I won't be advising that you follow any black-hat teaching methods; instead I'll focus on how to produce quality content in a way that the search engines not only appreciate but makes them sit up and listen.

That being said, what I will do is reveal many of the sneaky secrets that super-affiliates are using to stack the deck in their favor. These aren't black-hat strategies, more 'gaming' the system and working it in their favor. And you'll be able to copy them, (mostly) for free!

Whether you already have a whole gaggle of websites (is that the right term?) or this is your first one, I guarantee that if you religiously follow the well-worn steps laid out in this book you will once again return to the heady heights of *Googledom*. The beauty of these strategies is that they will create their own momentum. As Google begins to start trusting you, other sites start to notice, they link back to you, which in turn creates more trust with the search engines, and so on. Sort of like a self-fulfilling prophecy.

But what I won't be doing is creating an exhaustive list. I'm going to focus instead on those strategies that matter, laser-targeting the ones that will make real, tangible and noticeable results and leaving aside those that have little or no effect.

Yes, you could continue to fine-tune and tweak your sites to the nth degree in order to make tiny incremental notches up the Google ladder. And if that's what you want to go and do afterwards, then more power to your elbow. Be my guest. For me, life's just too short. I want the maximum gain for the minimum of pain. So I'll show you exactly where you need to be focusing your efforts to get the biggest bang for your buck.

I'll hold your hand and show you all the tried and tested techniques that worked for me and my websites with no-holds barred. And I'll teach you how to get yourself organized to be a lean, mean, money-making machine!

Together we'll propel your sites out of the doldrums to a point where they are once again trusted by Google and bringing you a very nice active or passive income. And once you know the formula, you simply rinse and repeat.

And the great thing about the majority of these strategies is that they create a kind of circular effect, where each strategy feeds into the next one, concentrating that link juice, constantly raising you through the ranks.

So be prepared for what I hope will be an enjoyable, worthwhile and profitable journey. Whether you're an internet marketer, a small business, or simply a hobbyist who wants to earn income from their site, passive or otherwise. There is something here for everyone.

I have tried to avoid being too prescriptive about exactly how to implement each of the areas – it will very much depend on your particular niche as to exactly how you want to do them or even in what order to do them.

You may even feel that a certain strategy does not easily lend itself to your particular topic in which case you can just skip it. But I'm hoping there will be enough in this book to give you those light bulb flashes in your head, where you see something you hadn't thought of before, or suddenly see how you can link one area to another and where you can't wait to get started to put your ideas into practice. These times I call the 'kid in the sweet shop moments'!

But I do ask that you follow the initial keyword investigation in Chapter 1 in order as there are certain key steps you need to follow here. After that, you can mix and match and pick the parts that are applicable to your own particular niche.

Also be prepared for some work – I'm not going to lie to you, you will need to put some effort in (is there anything that's really worthwhile that doesn't involve some effort?). We are talking perhaps an hour or two each day. But I hope it will also be enjoyable work. It's all about forward motion and keeping that momentum going.

And as you start to see the results of your efforts, you'll be amazed just how motivating this can be to keep driving yourself forward. Things may look a little bleak now but trust me, just follow the steps in this book and you will begin to see the light!

I have talked a lot about Google and it's certainly true that it does play a major part in getting your site to produce any income. But Google is not the only fruit. Many of the strategies in this book use many other crafty techniques to pull in the crowds, as well as your income. More on this later.

And by the end of this book you may even realize that all of these Google updates is actually a good thing for you. How? Think about it. Once you have implemented all the strategies here and demonstrated your quality to Google, you will start leap-frogging all the other lower quality sites as they increasingly fall beneath you. And who knows, you may even find that Google isn't so evil after all!

I hope you'll enjoy the journey with me. I aim to hold nothing back. So no more procrastinating and let's begin!

4. LET'S TALK ABOUT CONTENT

Now, more than ever before, content is king.

You can have thousands of related backlinks from authority sites, social bookmarks and press releases galore but if you're site contains scant, plagiarized, non-relevant content that no-one wants to read, then there's a high probability that neither will Google.

In fact, I estimate that content needs around 75% of your effort when putting your website together. If you're going to take one thing away from this book, this is the one. Your content and, to a lesser extent now, your keywords form the foundations of your site. So it needs to be right. And you need to be brutally honest with yourself about whether you have interesting, useful and relevant content on your site before progressing to any further chapters.

Have I stressed the importance of content sufficiently? OK, let's move on to how we achieve this.

We can think of content in terms of 2 things:

- Keywords (or keyphrases), and
- Content (the stuff on the pages)

Let's cover the keywords first...

5. KEYWORD RESEARCH

OK, I'm assuming you've all done some keyword research and know the basics so I just wanted to use this section as a quick sense-check.

The mistake many people make when selecting keywords (which used to include me by the way) is that they don't fully focus on their potential customer's needs.

The first thing you need to find out is: 'what are my potential customers actually going to be typing into the search engines?' In other words, what keywords will they be using?

Keyword is a bit of a misnomer; what we actually mean is keyphrases. After all, it would be extremely rare to rank for a single keyword, unless it's a highly unusual one!

So whether you're a small business, a hobby site or an affiliate marketer, you need to clearly identify exactly what your site is about and who your customers are.

Consider for a moment exactly what your goals for this site are.

Specifically:

- Who are my Audience?
- Are they part of a certain demographic? e.g. dog owners, car owners, women?
- What niche is my site focused on? e.g. dog grooming, English lessons, dating?

- Is my site local to a particular area, or does it have a global reach?
- What other 'on-topic' subjects are relevant to this niche that I can include as articles?

You should also at this point be able to write one or two sentences about your site, which concisely describes exactly what it's about.

For example:

"This website provides a resource for finding the best car insurance deals for women motorists in California.", or

"This website shows the best places to find guitar lessons in Orlando. There are also articles on how to play the guitar as well as videos and interviews with famous guitar players."

Once you've done this, you need to start brainstorming your key phrases. Just write down every possible phrase that you think is relevant to your site. And try to make them as relevant as possible – but don't go too far off-piste! You can use Excel, Notepad or even a pen and paper for this. I prefer to use Excel but it's up to you. Don't get hung up at this stage worrying how good the phrases are. Just start scribbling down all the phrases that comes to mind.

The subjects and hence phrases that tend to be the easiest to rank for are those which target either specific areas or specific demographics. The basic rule is: the smaller the area or demographic you target, the more chance you have of ranking for particular keyphrases. The area may be a state, a province, a city, whilst the demographic is your type of niche audience. Just try to focus on exactly who your users are and what you imagine they will be typing to get to you.

In the Guitar example, this might be:

- "Guitar Lessons in Orlando"
- "Electric guitar Lessons in Orlando"
- "Electric guitar lessons in Orlando"
- "Interviews with famous guitar players"
- "Video of Eric Clapton playing guitar"

At the end of this exercise, you should end up with a boatload of phrases of varying merit.

Now with this list in front of you, are there any that stand out as the phrase that best sums up your site? There are usually 1 or 2 that stand head and shoulders above the rest. This will be the phrase around which you will be building your website, so you need to ensure you get it right. I call this the headline phrase.

Panda/Penguin Alert - this headline phrase idea is key. Gone are the days when each web page was an island in itself and you tried to rank each page on its own a set of keywords. The new thinking is that this headline phrase becomes the topic around which the rest of your site revolves. Get this stage wrong, and you risk building your site on weak foundations. Subsequent keywords within your articles are less important. The important thing is that every article is 'on-topic'. So don't go putting Banjo articles on your Guitar website, unless you can properly justify it!

If there isn't an obvious keyphrase, then you'll need to go back and add more until you find one, but it's usually one of the first items on the list!

Now we need to see:

1. How many people are typing in this phrase, and
2. How much competition there is for it.

As I said, I am assuming you have your own methods for doing keyword research so I won't labor the point, but I find the easiest way to do this is to use the Google Keyword Tool.

It's a free tool, available at http://adwords.google.com. If you aren't already, you'll be asked to sign in with your Google account. If you don't have one then create one.

You can access the Keyword Tool outside of Adwords, but I strongly recommend that you create a Google account and use this address since you not only get more accurate results, but are also given suggested alternatives, which is great for generating additional keyword ideas.

Once in, type in your headline phrase in the 'Word or phrase' section. Depending on your target audience, you will also need to click on "Advanced Options and Filters" and choose the region of your potential customers. It's important to get this right or will get wildly misleading results! For instance, if you're targeting "Guitar Playing in Orlando", you don't want to see results from the UK!

After clicking the 'Search' button you should be presented with the results of your phrase, giving the amount of 'Competition', the 'Global Monthly Searches' and the 'Local Monthly Searches'.

Remember, if your website is targeting a particular area then just concentrate on the 'Local Monthly Searches' figure.

Now depending on the results you get, this may influence the direction your website takes. For instance, you may find that there are simply not enough Local Monthly Search results for your headline search term. Or that Google has an even better suggestion for you further down the results.

It's very difficult to say exactly what constitutes a good result without knowing the particular niche you are in and the area you are targeting, but as a general rule, if there are fewer than 100 results on 'Local Monthly Searches' and you are targeting local customers only, then you may need to think again about your niche phrase. If your target market is Global, you may have (and will need) many more results.

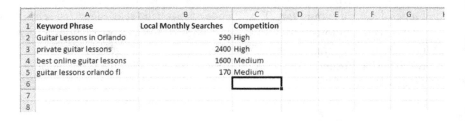

	A	B	C	D	E	F	G	
1	Keyword Phrase	Local Monthly Searches	Competition					
2	Guitar Lessons in Orlando	590	High					
3	private guitar lessons	2400	High					
4	best online guitar lessons	1600	Medium					
5	guitar lessons orlando fl	170	Medium					
6								
7								
8								

The important thing at this stage is to spend time working with this Tool until you have decided on your headline phrase, as well as at least 20 article keyphrase ideas. It can be a long process, but believe me, it will be worthwhile as they will be forming the foundations of your site.

Don't worry too much about the number of searches for the keyphrases of every article. Remember, we're writing on topics, not keywords. I'll be showing you plenty of strategies to get users back to you in the coming chapters. The most important thing is that you're happy with your headline phrase and that it has a reasonable number of results every month for your niche.

Panda/Penguin Alert – A quick note on keyword density of your various keyphrases: Don't worry too much about keyword density! Just make sure the keyphrase you have chosen for each particular page appears in your Title Tag, your H1 Tag, once at the beginning of your article and once at the end of your article. The phrase also doesn't have to be in the same word order – Google will work it out and it can often sound unnatural to do so. Don't go stuffing your keyphrase all over the place or Google will slap you for it. The same goes for your headline keyphrase – just use it on your main page in the same places and as a menu item. If your articles are all 'on-topic', believe me, Google will know!

Meta Tags

As for Meta Title and Meta Keywords tags, there's no harm sprinkling your keyphrases in here, and in my view they are better in than out. Just don't expect it to hold much weight with Google!

However, the *Meta Description* IS important as this is what appears in the Google results to your potential visitors. So make sure it has the relevant keyphrase, is short, snappy, and draws their attention.

See below for a good example of how Weightwatchers use their Meta Description:

Learn How to **Play Guitar** Series Lesson 1 - YouTube
www.youtube.com/watch?v=5dSp79TDWoc
Oct 20, 2007 - Uploaded by josephhkim
Learn how to **play guitar**. basic beginner course that increases in difficulty. acoustic, electric, and classical ...

More videos for **learning to play the guitar** »

If you've plugged all your keywords into Adwords and studied the results and you're still undecided at this stage about whether your niche will attract enough visitors, just put it on the back-burner for now. You can revisit after completing the next section, 'Evaluating the competition'. You'll find as your work through each chapter, that new ideas will naturally spring to mind so just keep going!

6. EVALUATING THE COMPETITION

It's so important to look at your competition. Would an athlete go into a race without knowing what their competitors are doing? Once you know what your competition is doing, you'll know what you need to do to beat them. But it's amazing how many people forget to do this step before plunging headlong into their website.

Remember, to outrun a bear you just need to run faster than the guy next to you!

At this point, I must mention a great free tool that you can use, which works with Mozilla Firefox (I find Firefox has so many more useful SEO tools than any other browser).

It can be found at:

http://www.quirk.biz/searchstatus

I strongly recommend you visit this site using Firefox and install. Once installed, it sits at the bottom right hand side of your browser and gives invaluable information about the competition.

For now, the important thing to look at is the item labeled 'PageRank'. If you visit a site and then hover your mouse over 'PageRank' whilst on the site, it will report the Google Page Rank for this page.

You can think of Page Rank as a measure of how much it trusts this page and is measured on a scale from 0 to 10. It's based on a very complicated algorithm, taking signals from a whole number of factors but it's a great indicator for measuring the strength of your competition based on Google's 'trust' of that site. Look at some of the major websites such as Wikipedia or Microsoft and you'll see they'll usually be between 7 and 9.

Ok, now go to Google and type in the headline keyphrase you've agreed upon.

Look at your first page of results and pick the top 5 or 6 results. Now open each one of them and take your time to browse through each site. Get a notepad and write down each one, making comments on each of the good bits and the bad bits about the site.

Does every site on that page:

- offer utterly comprehensive information on your niche?
- cover every subject on that topic, from every conceivable angle?
- have rich content and littered with fantastic videos, articles and interviews?
- offer a really amazing user experience?
- have a Google Page Rank of four or above?

Try to look at each site as objectively as you can and make plenty of notes. You should know enough about your chosen niche to be able to evaluate each site's worthiness. Are all five or six sites utterly unbeatable, or is their definite room for improvement for say, three of them?

Now do the same with your top 5 keyphrases (your best article keyphrases). How do the results look for these?

Remember, you don't need to beat all of them to still rank very highly. After all, you may be competing against a Wikipedia entry, or an article from MSN. These sites have very high Page Ranks of 8 or 9 and there is little point in picking a fight with them.

But the rest of them may only have a Page Rank of between zero and 3. If they do, and if you see chinks in their armor in terms of their content then they are eminently beatable with our strategies. Most of them will not be doing anything like the number of the things as comprehensively as you will be. So don't be put off by a few high-ranking sites.

However, if the answer to every question in the above points is a definitive 'yes' for every single site, then you may need to think about narrowing down your niche a little. Is there a gap in this niche to be exploited? (Use the Google Keyword Tool to assist you with this).

For instance, if your headline phrase was "Weight Loss", you'll see the kind of competition you're up against! Even my strategies would struggle to compete with this phrase (at least without spending a quite a bit of money!).

However, if we move to "Weight Loss for Women", and then maybe to "Weight Loss for Women over 50", the playing field starts to become much more level.

What you'll find is that as your niche begins to narrow, the quality of the sites will tend to diminish. With a little tweaking, you'll find that you'll hit that sweet spot where you'll see a page of results with terrible content or user experience that you just know you can better. This is especially true of local niches.

Now think about it, you only need to be on page one for a few phrases to gain incredible rankings and using my strategies you would have no trouble appearing on the first page, providing there are just a handful of lower authority sites. And once on that first page, my strategies will only continue to move you in one direction. And as the number of articles you post increases, the story just gets better and better!

So ask yourself if your niche is niche enough for you to compete with the first five to six results on Google. But don't be scared off by a couple of big boys. We can exploit those gaps!

Now let's move on to that all-important content.

7. CONTENT THAT RANKS

Hopefully by this point you should have a pretty good idea about:

- **Your headline keyphrase;**
- **At least 20 associated 'on-topic' keyphrases;**
- **The level of competition for these keyphrases.**

Why 20 articles? Not only does a good quantity of content ensure that you are covering the topic to a good standard, it can also be thought of as bet-spreading. After all, it's easier to get 10 people visiting 20 articles, than 200 people visiting 1!

If you're happy with all of the above, then congratulations, we're ready to begin putting the content together! If not, I recommend you go back and finish them off.

Ok, so let's say you've found your headline keyphrase and you're happy that it has enough monthly searches (local or global depending on your niche) to give you a nice slice of traffic, providing you can rank well enough for it. And that you have at least 20 articles to include on your chosen topic. You've also looked at your competition and know you can compete with a handful of them.

Now comes the difficult part – creating the content. I can't stress enough just how important this stage of the process is. In fact, do this right and you will have nailed 75% of what you need to do. Even if you have less backlinks than your competitor, the chances are that Google will still put you above them if it believes that you have provided the best answers in your niche; that's how important content is.

Panda/Penguin Alert - As part of the algorithm changes, Google realized that people can manipulate the system to gain more backlinks but that it's much harder to manipulate good content, without simply copying it from somewhere else, that is. So over time they are placing increasing value on this aspect. You really should view this as a good thing as many of your competition have been spending their valuable time just getting as many backlinks as they can, whether relevant or non-relevant. And Google is continually devaluing them – pathing the way for you to step in! They'll compare your content with theirs, see that it offers more and simply redirect the traffic to you.

Let's face it, without decent content, nobody is going to stick around on your site anyway. So make a commitment at this point that, for whatever niche you have chosen, that your content will be only of the highest quality.

Let's just say you have a niche on "How to build a website".

In order to be a great website, it must cover every base about how someone goes about building a website, including:

- How to choose the right domain;
- How to get a good hosting account;
- Articles on the various platforms you can build a site on, together with reviews, guides and tutorials;
- Articles on site design using CSS or HTML 5 perhaps, with video tutorials, and showcase sites;
- Articles and tutorials on PHP, WordPress, Javascript, etc.
- Plenty of video reviews and tutorials of the above;
- Maybe a forum on each of the different aspects of writing a website?
- Recommended reading and links to other related sites.

I hope you're getting the picture by now. Your site needs to cover your topic from every conceivable angle, and have answers to all your user's potential questions. And even when it doesn't have all of the answers, it knows someone who does and directs them accordingly. Once this is in place, you need much fewer backlinks to rank well (I'll be talking about backlinks in a later chapter).

Panda/Penguin Alert – stay on topic!
Your site must also not have irrelevant content. If the majority of your

articles was about search engine optimization or social marketing, then it wouldn't be fulfilling the needs of the user who has typed into Google: "How to Build a Website". Furthermore, the major search engines bots will land on your site, expecting to find articles on how to build a website, only to find a whole bunch of unrelated articles about something completely different and will mark your site accordingly. In other words, they certainly won't see yours as an authority site on this topic, so why on earth would they direct a user to you for this search term?

It's all about putting yourself into the shoes of your intended audience: what would you want to find if you landed onto a site on your niche? What would delight you and inspire you and encourage you to come back for more?

So many people fail to take note of this fundamental important point and it's a major factor in why so many websites fail. In order to rank well for your keywords, you need to have the best results for that particular search query.

In the previous chapter on keyword research, we've already looked at your competition and seen what they're doing. Look again and see how the top guys are doing it. Are they covering off all the topics? Can you get additional ideas from them for the kind of articles you should be including? Providing you don't have a really difficult niche, you should be able to brainstorm ideas for many more articles. Get them down now. When I'm researching ideas, I'll leave an Excel sheet open and just note any new ideas that I come across. Don't be too judgmental or choosy at this stage, just record them. You'll be surprised how much extra material you can come up with once you start flowing.

Later on, you can decide whether or not to retain certain articles based on their relevance or importance to your audience. Only then, when you have your pared down list of candidates and are fully happy with your list, do you put them in priority order of importance.

Let's face it, most people browsing the web have the concentration span of a goldfish so your main page needs to grab people's attention right away. It needs to project concisely exactly what it's about and demonstrate to your audience that this site really is what they're looking for. Think about what you can do to provide just that.

As well as simply post text, Google and your users love to see:

- Photos;
- Videos;
- Graphs and Charts;
- Reviews.

However, as ever, try to keep all of these as original as you possibly can. You may even be able to take your own photos or record your own videos. Google will love you for it!

Don't just paste a picture up you find on the web. Google will know and there may be either copyright issues or it will simply flag yours as being duplicate content. Use stock photography if you can't produce your own (see list of stock photography sites in the Appendix section).

Even if you do use stock photography, it's still preferable that you alter it in some way – you may want to add some text, change the background color or even adjust the brightness or saturation levels – but try to make it different enough to give Google the impression that it's unique. This can be done with all the major paint packages. I find Photoshop is best for this, or Photoshop Elements if you're on a budget.

And don't forget to complete the Alt tag for every image. This tells Google more about what the image is about. If you've ever looked at Google Images you'll see this in action. And if your images are unique enough, they will appear here, giving you an additional chance of users finding you!

OK, on to the main event – writing that content!

8. WRITING YOUR CONTENT

This is where many people freeze. But writing your articles doesn't need to be daunting; there are many options open to you. The good news is, you don't need to write all 20 articles in one go.

The important thing is to get organized and to start breaking things down into easy to digest bite-size chunks. If you've done the exercises up to now you should already know what 20 of your articles are going to be about. So let's get to the meat of the articles. And here's a great little exercise to help you put together the structure of each article:

The 'Keyword' Trick

Here's a great trick: for whatever headline keyphrase a particular articles will be covering, get a pen and paper and write down every single word that's relevant to that phrase. And make it as comprehensive as you possibly can.

So for example, with the keyphrase "How to install WordPress", you might have the following keywords: WordPress, install, PC, Mac, Windows 7, Windows XP, OSX, 3.51, version, zip, Fantastico, requirements, ftp, download, config, database, extract user, mysql, php, cpanel, etc..

You can get help with adding these keywords simply by looking at competitor's sites and seeing what they have. Thanks to the power of the internet, all the information you need is already out there, so use it!

When you have a fully comprehensive list, you now have a basis to start grouping some of these keywords together and splitting your article into logical sub-headings. These may be:

"How to Download WordPress", "How to create a WordPress Database" "How to Use cPanel to Install WordPress", etc.

Your finished article should have every word included in the initial list, together with nice logical sub-headings for your visitors to follow. And you'll probably think of many more as you go and your juices start flowing.

Can you see just how powerful this method is? Google is actively looking for clues as to how much of an authority you are on this topic. It will be looking at your headings and keywords for these clues and each time it puts a little tick in its box, you become that little more trustworthy and move up those rankings.

As clever as Google is, it doesn't understand all of the nuances of the English Language (or any other language for that matter). For instance, it doesn't do a great job understanding irony, sarcasm or even if you're being witty and telling a particularly funny joke. So it has to look for clues in your content through sets of keywords it's expecting to see on a given topic. These are its signals. It will then tick these off against its own little checklist. Basically, the more things it ticks off, the more it likes your content. The more it likes your content, the more it likes your site!

OK let's just quickly recap where we are so far. You should by now have:

1. Decided on your niche and decided that there is both a market for it and that there is not too much competition;
2. Agreed on your Headline Keyphrase;
3. Agreed on at least 20 articles that are on-topic and are what the user will expect to find;
4. Agreed that the articles cover at least a good proportion of the chosen niche's topic;
5. For each article you have chosen a list of keywords that need to appear in each;
6. For each article you have constructed a logical set of subheadings that cover all of the aspects of this keyphrase.

Writing the articles

Now on to writing the articles. The exercises you have been doing so far will stand you in good stead for getting that content done. You should now know what articles you will be writing and exactly what sections you will have in each article a direct result of your exhaustive list of keywords.

If you have followed all the exercises up to now, you will have effectively completed a skeleton framework of your entire website! Hopefully you can see just how useful this is: you are no longer simply staring at a black screen and praying for divine inspiration!

Filling in the blanks

There are a number of ways to get your articles nailed. You can:

- Write them yourself;
- Record them yourself and then type them yourself (or use a dictation program);
- Record & get them transcribed using an outsourced transcriber;
- Outsource them.

When writing this book, I thought about all the things I would need to write about, the sections I would need, getting a decent cover designed, getting it published to Amazon, feeding the Amazon site to my own website, etc. All these seemingly endless tasks can easily overwhelm you if you don't break things down.

So it's important to write down each step, and commit to doing at least one action a day. For me it may be writing a chapter, or part of a chapter, or simply doing research for a particular section. So this huge, daunting task simply became a series of daily tasks (no matter how small) that I could tick off each day with a grin of smug self-satisfaction! The important thing is to be further forward at the end of the day than you were at the beginning of the day. Just keep that forward motion going!

Once you've completed a couple of articles, things will start to become much easier, I promise. Who knows, you may even start enjoying it! Just set aside an hour or two each day, instead of watching TV. Remember, you have your list of keywords, titles and subheadings, so a lot of the legwork has already been done. Depending on how you've structured your subheadings, some may only require to be one of two paragraphs long.

A word on outsourcing

I strongly recommend writing the first set of articles yourself before considering outsourcing. That way you'll get a feel for how it's done and you'll begin to take real ownership of your site, instead of being simply an onlooker. You'll also be much better at knowing what style of articles you'll need going forward and be able to provide your outsourcer with much more detailed instructions – crucial for producing quality articles. And if you do go down the outsourcing router it's always worth paying a little more to get decent quality – as with most things in life, you get what you pay for!

I'll be providing a list of good article writers and transcribers at the end of this book.

Other considerations

Ok, hopefully you now know the importance of great content. But once you have this content, you need to ensure that Google and the other search engines can find you.

The main 'on-page' indicators that Google looks for to understand exactly what your site is about are the:

- Page Titles (what appears at the top of the browser),
- Headings and Sub Headings (H1 and H2 tags),
- Links (on the menu, sidebar or inside the article itself), and
- Keywords within the content.

So don't forget to ensure that you have the correct keyphrases for each article plugged into these areas. You'll be surprised that many people simply don't use these tags correctly and without them Google will have no clear idea whether your website is completely 'on-topic'. So fill them in with care and leave them in no doubt that you are!

This also acts as a double-whammy as it not only helps Google find you, but also demonstrates to your users as they browse your article titles, headings and links at a glance that this is absolutely what they are looking for.

For example, if you're chosen niche was 'How to Build Websites in WordPress', this will most likely be your main page title. You might then have the following elements on your main page:

Title: "How to Build Websites with Wordpress"
Main Heading: "How to Build Wordpress Websites"
Sub heading 1: "Getting started with Wordpress"
Sub heading 2: "Putting your first website together"

Sub Heading 3: "How to Install Wordpress"
Sidebar Link 1: "Where to Find Wordpress"
Sidebar Link 2: "The Best Wordpress Plugins"
etc.

Depending on how you design your site, will alter how and where the various elements appear. However the key rule is the same: make sure you include your main keyphrase in the Title and Main heading (the words within the keyphrase can even be in a different order - and yes, Google is clever enough to work this out!) and then for each page use some elements of that keyphrase in your sub-headings and links. That way Google will both know what your site is about and that it is remaining 'on-topic' and is therefore a high-quality site. And don't just litter the page with "How to Build Websites with Wordpress"! Google will just see you as spammy. Keep your articles as natural as you can. Once at the beginning and once at the end is fine. Your related keywords you compiled and included at the beginning of this chapter will do the rest.

Panda/Penguin Alert - Google is always looking to see if your pages are all 'on-topic'. So in the sidebars, keep the links relevant to the articles the visitors are reading. They are far more likely to click on them, which means they'll stay on your site for longer.

Generally speaking, articles containing upwards of 700 words tend to rank the best. However, there is no hard and fast rule on this and it very much depends on the subject you are writing about. As long as you are covering all the content, then it's absolutely fine that some articles are much shorter. If you have covered everything in your article, then the worst thing you can do is to waffle on simply to make your word count.

OK now your content's beginning to flow, it's time to start making the magic happen!

9. JOINING THE CONVERSATION

We've all been to those parties – everyone's in huddles chatting away and you're standing there in the corner on your own, nursing your Gin and Tonic.

OK, maybe it was just me.

Panda/Penguin Alert - if there's one thing Google hates, it's online social pariahs. To them, that is just what a static website represents. They hate the kind of websites that are simply stuck up with a few information pages, that are never updated and left to rust. There they remain, not contributing anything to the web community and not joining in with the crowd. These kind of sites may have gotten away with it pre-Panda and Penguin, but those days are long gone. So if you haven't done so already, you need start joining in the conversation.

Like it or not, Twitter and Facebook are here to stay and being social is a big positive indicator to Google towards the ranking of your website.

You may be in a niche you absolutely love, and adore conversing endlessly with your followers, in which case, carry on doing it! But what if you're not one of those kind of people and you simply can't see yourself as a prolific tweeter? Your heart may sink at the very thought of tweeting and if you think that's you, there's some good news: there are ways around it.

It doesn't need to be tiresome, and it doesn't have to involve Tweeting or updating your Facebook status every minute of the day.

But there are certain things you need to do as a bare minimum in order to send out the right sorts of signals to Google et al.

To an extent, Google wants what we want: they want to know there's a 'buzz' around your website, something that keeps your users coming back for more, whether it's to look at your fresh and exciting content or to contribute to the latest discussion. Twitter and Facebook is simply another conduit, facilitating this process, a way of bringing visitors back to you for more through social interaction.

So you need to start thinking of it as a win-win situation: your visitors will love you, and Google will also love you!

However, if you do think that you fall into that socio-phobe category, there are basically 3 main sites where you need to concentrate your social marketing efforts. Sure there are others, but these will cover 95% of the required Google juice:

- Google+,
- Twitter and
- Facebook

Out of all of them, Google+ is arguably the most important (I wonder why??). So if you haven't already sign up and get accounts to all three of these sites. Go on, do it. Now. I'll wait.

Panda/Penguin Alert

And when you create the accounts, ensure you complete as much information in your profile as you can, and keep the information consistent throughout. Google constantly trawls these sites and pieces together a profile of you. If anything doesn't chime as being true, it can erode your trust levels. Don't take that risk.

Then, as you complete each article and post it, simply:

- Tweet about it – "Hey check out my amazing new article on how to install WordPress!"
- Facebook it – one or 2 paragraphs on your article.
- Google+ about it – ditto.

And don't forget to link your various social accounts together. For instance, within Twitter there's an option to connect to your associated Facebook account. Do this and you can also send any tweets you do automatically to your Facebook blog; a nice way of killing two birds with one stone!

However, it's always a good idea to add a new entry of your own in both Facebook and Google+ each time you post a new article, maybe just a paragraph or two. Keep them slightly different, and if you can add some images, videos or links to other related sites, so much the better.

And for heaven's sake, don't forget to include a link back to your original article! Doing each of these things will give you 3 damn good backlinks every time you create an article!

All this should only add around 15-30 minutes of your time, and it's time very well spent. This activity will be viewed by Google that you are socially active. Not to mention also giving you those all-important backlinks.

Another way of adding friends to your social circles is to start following others. So spend a few minutes each morning following some relevant people on Twitter, liking someone on Facebook and adding to your Circles on Google+. You'll find that your efforts will start to get reciprocated by others following you. Give and you shall receive!

Pinterest is also a growing social site, that allows you to 'Pin' items of interest. However, this type of site tends to lend itself to niches that have a visual aspect to them, so this may or may not fit into your particular niche, but definitely something to bear in mind.

What you need to try to avoid is constantly signing up to the 'next big thing' and find that all your time is swallowed up. Keep things simple and just concentrate on ticking these 3 sites over each day. But don't let them dominate your life!

Be a Follower!

OK you've set the foundations in place now. You have great articles on your site, and you are talking about them on Twitter, Facebook and Google+. But nobody is listening to you. When you first start off you're like one of the Borrowers, desperately shouting and waving from the skirting boards: no-one is listening and everyone is ignoring you, busy doing their own things and oblivious to your presence.

So how do we get people to listen to us? To begin with, we simply follow!

A great place to start following, is on each of these 3 sites – Twitter, Facebook and Google+.

For Twitter, it's simply a matter of finding like-minded people or people/organizations who may be interested in your niche and clicking the 'Follow' button. You'll probably find that for every 10-20 follows you do, you may get a single follow back. But this is fine. We're simply starting the ball rolling for now.

Now do the same with Facebook and Google+ and join targeted fanpages, profiles and Circles of your target audience. And once accepted, provide useful, valuable comments (or even just a little flattery!). Believe me these will go a long way. OK, you're starting the conversation. You'll gradually get a slow drip-drip of followers back at the beginning, but don't worry if you're not inundated with followers at this stage. Remember, it's all about that steady, forward motion.

Social Bookmarking

This is another area that has been abused in the past and that Google is onto post Panda and Penguin. But if used correctly, it's a great way of getting free backlinks and traffic back to your site.

The trick is to have a selection of your posts reworded and with a slightly different title posted to each of these sites. Ideally, even at the reworded posts should be a different for each social bookmarking site. In the past, posts were simply copied and pasted across every single site and, as we know, Google no longer tolerates this!

Ensure that any links back to your site go directly to the page in question to keep things relevant to both the user and to Google.

These articles do not need to be a very long (200 to 300 words will be fine). And try to keep the articles as well as your titles as interesting as possible since the average user has a very short concentration span. You need to grab their attention.

There are many social bookmarking sites around but I concentrate on just for the following two, which gives me the most bang for my buck. These are:

- Digg.com, and
- Reddit.com

These sites are also great for getting local traffic as you also have the ability to put your content into areas of your own locality as well as certain niches. So give some thought as to exactly what category and area you want to put your articles into.

There are others, including Delicious, Folkd, Diigo and StumbleUpon, and if you have time, by all means post to these sites as well. After all, the more sites you post to, them all back links as well as potential traffic you will get.

There is also Pinterest (pinterest.com), a relatively young site which is becoming very popular. With this site, you 'Pin' areas of interest you find from around the web to different 'Boards'. These may be in the form of pictures, videos or simply links to other sites you find interesting . This site tends to lend itself very well to the more visual niches, such as photography, marketing, food, fashion and arts & crafts. You need to decide if your particular niche will be a fit here.

There is potentially a lot of power in social bookmarking sites: If someone likes your article, they bookmark it and other people see it, who may then also choose to bookmark it, and so on. This can provide an awful lot of backlinks to your site, not to mention great exposure. Not only that, but sites like Digg and Reddit 'mirror' the articles you post onto a whole host of other sites, dramatically increasing your exposure.

As you can see, you can really get a lot of traffic to your site simply be posting great articles to Digg, Reddit et al, so give some serious thought to doing this after each article you create.

Article Directories

As well as social bookmarking sites, there is a whole plethora of article directories, including:

- WordPress.com
- Tumblr.com
- Hubpages.com
- Livestrong.com
- Ask.com
- Ezinearticles.com
- Livejournal.com

The list goes on and on, into the hundreds! But the above are the current leading ones and where your efforts will be best rewarded.

As with the social bookmarking sites, you can put summaries of your articles up here, linking back to the original article on your site. Not only will they very quickly be found by Google and other search engines, if they are of good quality, they will provide a lot of traffic back to your site.

Again, these don't all need to be overly long, but simply need to have content that will entice your readers. And nor do you need to do all of them at once. Start with one or two and add to them gradually.

The top social bookmarking and article directory sites are both what I call 'self-ranking'. This means that not only do they provide good backlinks to your site and are searchable within the sites themselves, their results also often appear very high up in the Google search results in their own right. This makes them very valuable to you and you'll be surprised how many people disregard them when considering their overall ranking strategy.

With most of these sites, you don't need to have great long re-worded essays in all of them. Often you can simply mention your main website article, along with a flavor to your readers of what it's about. Just enough to entice them back to your site.

Once you get good at it you should be able to fly through 3 social bookmarking sites and 3 article directories in less than an hour per article. And believe me, it will be an hour well spent!

Press Releases

This is very much an optional step but one worth considering later on, particularly if you feel that your niche offers something newsworthy to say.
The two leading press release news sites are:

- Prweb.com, and
- Prnewswire.com

These sites, for a fee, will distribute your stories to all the major news networks, locally, nationally and sometimes internationally depending on the topic. If the news agencies deem the stories newsworthy, they will then post them on their own sites.

Submissions to the sites is not free but in the right niche, and with the right story it can lead to a tremendous amount of exposure.

You may be thinking: "but how can my niche possibly be worthy of showing up on CNN?". Well, you'd be surprised. For instance, many enterprising weight-loss affiliates are producing articles on the latest fat-reducing fads and then inserting links to their own sites.

Panda/Penguin Alert

My only caveat is that it can be open to abuse, and may eventually be slapped down by Google unless they get their respective acts together. For example, affiliates of Viagra will pay for many press releases about their own products, and these are then appearing on many news sites, shamelessly plugging their wares. Not good. But surprisingly, for now, Google appears to still be pushing these results very high up in the rankings!

So very much an optional step but something worth considering for the future. Get creative and see if there's some angle for your own niche that you could try to make newsworthy!

10. BECOMING AN EXPERT

Pre Panda and Penguin, it really wasn't so important to be an 'expert' in Google's eyes. In the old days, it was simply a question of getting as many backlinks as you could, regardless of quality; whoever had the most links tended to get the best rankings. The trouble with this method of scoring websites, was that the site could still have been of very low quality and it simply wasn't serving the visitors with quality information.

Panda/Penguin Alert

As a backlash to this, Google has now changed all that and being an expert can out-trump a hundreds of low-quality backlinks every time.

By following these steps, you'll stand out from the crowd, not only with Google, but to your visitors too. And with this perception of expertise comes a great deal of trust, which in turn will dramatically increase both your traffic and your conversions. If Google sees you as being trustworthy, they are going to be much more likely to display your site above many others they view as less respectable!

So how do you become an expert?

Gravatar

This first step is to show everyone that you're a real person. The best way of doing this is by going to Gravatar (www.gravatar.com) and uploading an image of yourself. You'll need to create an account first and your details will need to be the same as those on your website. And make sure you use the same e-mail address. Once done, you'll find that the 'Avatar' you've created will magically follow you around the web! When you comment on forums or subscribe to other sites, an image of your lovely face will appear! This saves an awful lot of effort uploading your image on every site you subscribe to. So I recommend, if you haven't already, to go and do this now!

Become an Author!

Google have created a nifty, and surprisingly little-known feature known as 'Google Authorship'. This doesn't mean you have to go away and write a book! It simply signifies you as the author of your own website.

Have you ever done a search in Google and seen someone's picture underneath the search result? This is known as a 'Rich Snippet' and Google appends this to your search result. That's Google Authorship for you. And whenever such an image appears, it has the effect of engendering a great deal of trust with the searcher. And it's been shown that users are much more likely to click on a result with such an image than one without. In fact, one study found that the number of clicks on such links increased by 150%!

And it's fairly easy to set up Authorship on your own website. You'll need to use the Google+ account that you set up in the previous chapter (this will be a Gmail address).

Then go to https://plus.google.com/authorship, enter the email address you want to have as your primary address and click on the button 'Sign Up for Authorship' and follow the instructions.

Once you've verified your email address, if you then edit your profile section within Google+, you'll find a section called 'contributor to' (currently under the 'About' section). Here you simply edit this and enter your website address and according to Google you should be good to go.

However, you also need to now add some code to your website, preferably in the Header section, so it appears for every Google result.

If you're using WordPress, then one good plugin you can use to do this is called "Google Plus Authorship". Once installed, go to your Profile (in Users section of your Admin console). Here you'll find a new section called Google Plus profile information. You then paste in your Google+ identifier into the Google Plus Profile URL box.

To get this, I find the best way is log in to Google+ and click on 'Profile' link on the left-hand bar (unless they change the design!). Then copy the URL in the address bar, leaving out the 'posts' part. It should be in

the form:
https://plus.google.com/110430920700514869471

or something similar.

To test it's working, you can go to:

http://www.google.com/webmasters/tools/richsnippets

and type in the URL of one of your blog posts. It should then show you a sample search result of your website along with your mugshot at the bottom. A typical result with a photo will look as below:

Preview

Terms | The Only Place To Go for SEO
www.onlyplacetogo.com/terms/
 by James Green - More by James Green
The excerpt from the page will show up here. The reason we can't show text from your webpage is because the text depends on the query the user types.

This is why it's so important to keep everything uniform in terms of your name, emails address and bio, wherever you travel on the web.

Blog commenting

This can be a contentious area as it is still often abused by spammers; however it can still be very powerful providing it is used correctly.

Pre Panda and Penguin, people wanting to get free backlinks would fly around from forum to forum, sticking any old comments up there and in return Google would reward them by rank them higher. However, Google no longer gives these backlinks anywhere near the weight they used to. But this strategy isn't about Google, it's about getting yourself out there and showing everyone what an expert you are!

Remember that what they are looking for now is quality and, more importantly, relevant backlinks. So commenting on blogs is still a very effective strategy you can employ if you are a real expert in your arena or even simply have an interest in your topic and feel that you can provide value in your comments. Think about what blogs may be relevant to your niche and then do some searching on Google and get commenting.

Armed with your new Gravatar, you can start to build a visible presence by helping people out with your expert advice. And yes, you may be able to get some back-links as well along the way. But don't force the issue, sticking any old comments up there with a scattering of links back to your site without expecting a negative response from the forum moderator! Provide well thought out and clear advice, and just put a backlink in your bio. If you feel it's relevant later on to link back to your site, then do this once you're more established on that site, say after 5 or 6 posts. Your links are far more likely to be accepted then.

And just as important as backlinks is having an expert presence. If you do, you'll find that others will seek you out for advice. And thanks to Google Authorship, they'll have a much easier time finding you!

You'll be ahead of the crowd. Remember lots of people follow some of the strategies in this book, but very few do ALL of them. Do them and you'll be ahead of the game.

Becoming a real author!

Question: does your particular niche lend itself easily to writing books on your topic? We're not talking great rollercoaster novels here. Think reports rather than books that you can publish to Amazon.

Gone are the days of spending months or years putting your content together and then more years trying to find a suitable publisher to approve and print your work. Enter Amazon KDP (kdp.amazon.com). Depending on the size of the book (report!) you plan to write it may take as little as a month from idea to published book, sitting proud on Amazon, earning you a nice little passive income on the side.

Publishing a book is a great way of becoming an expert. You leverage the power of Amazon. People tend to trust authors more than abstract websites. It's like Google Authorship but with a v8 turbo-charger attached! There seems to be a perception that you are more of an expert if you've spent months sweating over a book!

This topic is outside the scope of this book but I hope to be putting together lots of material on the various strategies of producing books for Amazon on my website over the coming months, so please visit regularly for the latest updates. I may also bring out a book on it!

Definitely something worth bearing in mind though, since Google loves Amazon in terms of ranking and this too has that magic circular effect:

- If a visitor searches on Amazon on a keyphrase your book magically shows up on page one.
- If they search on a keyphrase on Google, your book magically shows up on page one.
- People buy your book and from there they may visit your website.
- And if they visit your website first, they may just end up buying your book via a well-placed link!

Not only that, but when you publish a book, Amazon gives you your very own author page. So if someone likes your book, they can read about you and then find other books you've written. You can even put an RSS feed from your own website into this author page, which in turn feeds back to your own website. And the circle continues to revolve…

In a similar same way to Google authorship, the Google search results containing a book look so much more enticing as it shows the number of reviews received as stars inside, which can be a strong 'click-thru' signal. Think about it, if you saw two results, and one contained a 4 or 5 star rating inside it whereas the other simply contained text, which result would you be more likely to click on?

In addition don't forget that people also use Amazon as a search engine as well when looking for information almost secondary to Google, so having a book will dramatically increase your odds of being found too.

Expertise is all about perception. So think about how you can become an 'expert' in your own field.

11. HOW TO MAKE YOUR WEBSITES 'STICKY'

Keeping your site Fresh

What tends to happen when users develop websites is they are super-enthusiastic at the beginning of the project but, as time goes on, this enthusiasm tends to wane. There are however, a few tricks for keeping it fresh for both Google and your visitors.

Once you have the initial articles on your site, you need to start thinking about future content. Google simply wants to see signs of activity. This may or may not involve posting articles. It may be simply updating or editing your existing posts, or responding to comments on your site.

As you progress, you may even want to start outsourcing some of your posts. If you do, make sure they remain of excellent quality. It's surprisingly inexpensive to do this and can save a lot of your valuable time.

See my Appendix for my favorite outsourcing sites.

Schedule your Content

As eager as you are to get lots of articles up there in one go, it would be far better to simply post one every few days. Google is continually looking at the activity on your website and if it suddenly sees 10 more articles appear, followed by months of inactivity, it's going to become suspicious. So keep that momentum going and simply add to them over time.

You need to be aiming to add a new post every week as a bare minimum, and preferably 2 to 3 posts per week. WordPress allows you to schedule your posts, so you may have inspirational days when you are able to write a whole bunch of posts in one go. If you do, don't just publish them all at once. Schedule each one to be published, say, 3 days apart. If you have 10 posts, this will keep your site updating and looking fresh as a daisy for a whole month! This looks far more natural than a whole bunch of articles appearing in one go, then nothing!

Twitter Feed

Another way of showing fresh content to your users is to put your Twitter Feed onto your site. That way every Tweet you do will be updating your page!

Respond to comments

If you use a WordPress site, which I strongly recommend you do, your posts will also accept comments from visitors, which you can then reply to – a great way to show both your users and Google that the site is staying fresh. You most likely won't have any comments at the beginning. However, there is a crafty technique the super-affiliates use here to effectively comment on their blogs – what I would call a 'gray-hat' strategy. More on this in the 'Super-Affiliate Secrets' section!

You'll be surprised how with regular updates just how fast your site can grow. For instance, even if you only did one article as week, that's 52 articles! If you have just 7 visitors to each article a day, that's 364 visitors a day! Having a site with 52 articles is a bit like having 52 lottery tickets! And the great thing is, you can have as many lottery tickets as you want... for free!

Provide Good Navigation

There's nothing worse than landing on a site and not knowing what it's about or which way to go. Put yourself in your customer's shoes – what sort of experience would you like to have on your site? Try to avoid lots of sub menus where users are required to drill down three levels of menus to get to the good stuff. They will make their mind up pretty quickly about your website so grab them straightaway with relevant messages and articles.

And keep things as simple as possible.

The key is to ensure that your readers are always seeing the most relevant information to the article they are reading. You'll see this in action on Wikipedia – when you read a particular article, you'll see loads of links to every topic closely related to that subject. This increases the 'click-thru' rate and increases the time they'll spend on the site.

If you're using WordPress a great tip is to use content-sensitive widgets that show content closely related to the main content. The 'Related Posts' widget is a good example. If you're good at coding in WordPress then go to http://codex.wordpress.org/conditional_tags - this shows you how you can control the appearance of certain posts only on certain pages.

Another way if to ensure you categorize each post and then use the 'Posts by Category' widget to display the most posts only in that category.

** Panda/Penguin Alert **

Something Google now holds great store in is something called the Bounce Rate of a website. This is the amount of time a given visitor spends on your site as a whole. Every time Google sees users landing on your site and then instantly leaving, this will increase your Bounce Rate, which in turn will have an adverse effect on your rankings. If, on the other hand, they see users clicking onto different parts of your site and spending time and generally just 'hanging out' there, your Bounce Rate will decrease and your rankings will increase.

Include a Forum

Having a forum on your site encourages visitors to remain on the site for longer and to keep returning, time after time, and can make your website very sticky indeed.

But you will need to give some thought as to whether your particular niche easily lends itself to having a forum – not all do.

You'll also need to consider that, as a moderator, there will be quite a time commitment required in both setting up a forum page as well as moderating and approving comments and accounts, particularly as the site grows.

Use Videos

Another way to decrease your Bounce Rate is to put rich content on your site. As YouTube shows, people love videos. If you can make your own videos or put up your own graphics, whether it's charts or spreadsheets, then your visitors will lap them up.

Site Visitor Dwell Times

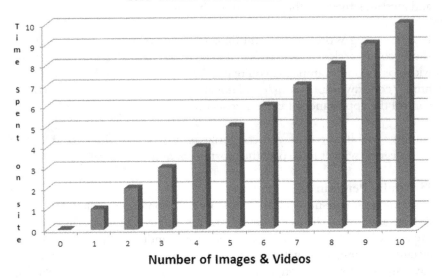

See how your eyes were drawn to this completely meaningless chart?

Just remember to make them as unique as possible.

Website Performance

Users don't have time to spend waiting for your site to load; and if it takes too long they will simply go elsewhere. So make sure you choose a good hosting provider and that your videos and images are well optimized. A typical jpg image should be no more than 40k in size.

A great site to use for increasing the performance of your site, particularly on WordPress sites, is GTMetrix (gtmetrix.com). The site is free and it will carry out a performance test on your site. Just type in your URL and it will then give you specific easy to follow steps to increase its performance. The results are nearly always pretty dramatic: on my own WordPress sites I will often go from a C or D to a B+ or an A. It takes around 15-20 minutes to do the required tasks from beginning to end; time well spent I think you'll agree! Your visitors will certainly thank you for it.

Test Your Links

It may sound obvious but it's worth spending time going through all the links on your site and make sure they all go where they're supposed to.

There's nothing worse than a broken link for putting off visitors. And while you're at it, check your grammar and spelling, another big turn-off to visitors: it can indicate that you don't care about your content.

So remember my FAIRER acronym, keep your site:

- Functional,
- Active,
- Interesting,
- Fresh,
- Rich,
- Enjoyable, and
- Relevant.

Do this, not for Google but for your visitors, and they'll keep coming back for more!

12. SUPER-AFFILIATE SECRETS

If you want to know how to rank well in Google, ask a super-affiliate! What is a super affiliate? Affiliates simply act as conduits between potential buyers and sellers. They grab the user's attention and then direct them to the sellers, who will then hopefully make a sale. When they do, they give an agreed commission to the affiliate.

Super affiliates have taken this to the next level, and usually own many sites, each one making its own passive income, and often assisted (and sometimes even run) by a number of outsourced individuals. Since they rely so heavily on traffic to generate sales, they are constantly coming up with new tricks to get most visitors to their site.

In an ideal world, sites would all naturally rise to the top like cream on milk, and to an extent and given time, this is increasingly true post Panda and Penguin. And by following the previous strategies, you will reach high up that ladder over time. But super-affiliates are impatient creatures and want high rankings now!

And after interviewing a good number of these super-affiliates, they have revealed some real hidden treasures.

The 'question-answer' trick

– Blog commenting

For some reason, nobody wants to be first person to comment on blog posts. It's like being the first person to put their hand up in class. Everyone waits for everyone else.

So the super-affiliate will register a number of different email accounts, ask a question with one account, and answer it with another!

Once a user sees a few comments, they are much more likely to post a comment of their own. Google also sees this activity on the site and in turn, raises it up a little, and everyone's happy!

– Ask.com

A similar trick can be done here: pose a question with one account, and answer it with another! This time, you simply add a backlink to a page on your own site.

But you have to be canny when doing this. It's important not to be too obvious, and to provide value in your answers.

With both of the above, sites are latching onto such tricks and may even be able to detect if you are in fact the same person. A much better method is to post a question, and then have a friend answer it, along with your all-important backlink! That way, there's no easily detectable connection.

Buying high-quality Domains

The thing about super-affiliates is that they tend to have a lot of money; this gives them terrific buying power. They know that Google now holds a lot of store in high quality, relevant backlinks, with a strong emphasis on relevancy.

So they'll hop onto a domain auction site such as freshdrop.net and bid on a site that is due to expire soon. They will target only high Page Rank sites of at PR 3. These will already have many incoming backlinks pointing at them. This becomes their 'sister site' and is cunningly adapted to link back to the main site, which then immediately grows in stature!

If you're patient and are prepared to bide your time, it's really quite surprising just how little money these domains can cost. Yes, you can pay in the thousands for some domains, but some PR2 sites, with maybe ten thousand backlinks can be picked up for a little as $100. How much time and money would you need to spend to get 10,000 backlinks?

There are thousands of domains expiring every day and there is a very good chance of you too picking up a terrific bargain.

A quick word on domain names in general – if you possibly can, always go for a .com domain as your first choice, followed by a .net domain. These still rank the best. The exception is for local businesses or where you're targeting traffic specific to a certain country. So if your customer target is the UK, then a .co.uk domain will hold much more weight.

It's also not as important anymore to have a domain name with your keyphrase inside it. However, if you can squeeze it in, then so much the better. Also avoid hyphens if you can, unless the phrase easily lends itself to them e.g. time-saving or eye-catching.

Finally, make sure you don't choose domains that can be read in different ways. A good illustration of this is the rather unfortunate Susan Boyle Twitter hashtag for a bash she was holding to promote her new album:

#susanalbumparty – this was seriously misinterpreted by many readers! However, it did get many thousands of hits!

Paying for Backlinks

Another strategy super-affiliates employ is to buy backlinks from other related sites. This could be in the form of hard cash, but other incentives may also be offered, such as a high PR backlink to their own site in return. Sometimes even both.

Once they have the high PR Domain as a bargaining chip, negotiating becomes much easier!

What they won't often do is give you a reciprocal backlink from their main site. That is, "you give me a link to my main site and I'll give you a link back to your site from my main site."

** Panda/Penguin Alert **

The reason they do this is that Google now sees reciprocal links almost as cancelling each other out. It's much more powerful to get a backlink from a high PR site and not to give one back. It looks less contrived in Google's eyes.

This is where their sister site comes in. They offer a link from their sister site in return for a link to their main site. Clever, huh?

Acquiring competitor sites

This is the next logical step – by simply buying their competition, they gain all their existing customers as well! But often very costly, and probably not recommended at this stage!

YouTube Marketing

We all know people love watching videos more than reading content. We also know how much Google likes YouTube (especially since they bought it!). So a highly effective route to generating huge amounts of traffic back to your site is to post YouTube videos on topics in your niche. Excellent areas are reviews and 'how-to' videos.

If you search for pretty much anything nowadays on Google, you'll see a YouTube result almost always on page one. And that could be you!

At the time of writing, YouTube has just reached 1 billion viewers, with one in two internet users using it on a regular basis, so you can see the its power!

The super-affiliate has known this for some time now and YouTube is filled with affiliates pushing their wares. But many videos can be of a poor quality. Which is where you can step in!

A few tips on making YouTube Videos:

- Keep each video under 5 minutes long. If you have more to say, then produce a series.
- Rehearse before you record. Practice makes perfect. Use an autocue if talking to camera (or ask someone to hold up cards!).
- If you're using a PowerPoint presentation, use plenty of bullet points and expand on them.
- Speak clearly and don't mumble.
- Invest in a good microphone (and video camera, if using one).
- Have an introduction and a summary at both ends.
- Don't forget to put your website link below your video.

A common objection to video marketing is that people don't like to put themselves in front of a camera. If this is the case, then depending on the niche you are in, it may be possible to use a PowerPoint presentation, or to demonstrate a website or program on your own PC. To do this you'll need some screen capture software such as Camtasia or Camstudio (the latter being free). You will then simply need PowerPoint or whatever program you plan to show, along with a good quality microphone.

This type of marketing can be extremely powerful and is very worthwhile looking into. I will be including articles on how to get the best out of YouTube marketing on my website. I see it very much as an under-rated and under-used medium.

Email Marketing

Email marketing is another very powerful medium since the audience you are targeting is already 'warm' and interested. After all, they have subscribed to receive your emails in the first place and are already sitting up and listening. With such a captive audience, the super-affiliate will send 'offers' along with informational emails. People will have subscribed to get a free report, or a special offer and will then join the email treadmill.

This really is a 'win-win' situation for them since it's not only possible to insert links back to the main site, but also to embed affiliate links directly into the emails, generating instant income should they subsequently purchase from the link.

The great thing about email marketing is you can continue to market to this captive audience ad-infinitum, which is exactly what super-affiliates do! My favorite tool for this is Aweber. They do charge around $19 per month for the service however, so you may want to wait until you are getting a good level of traffic first.

Outsourcing

Outsourcing is the super-affiliate's dirty secret. It's what enables them to produce many rich, content-filled websites in a matter of days. As with most things in this world, you pretty much get what you pay for with outsourcing.

I think the only exception to this for me has been Fiverr.com, which has been a revelation. Here you can get just about any simple task done for only $5!

I have been very pleasantly surprised by the quality of work from this site; maybe I've just been lucky and chosen the right people. In fact, I used someone on Fiverr.com to design my book cover and received a 2D and 3D version in the mix! For an additional $5 I also was supplied with the original Photoshop source image – great if you want to redesign it yourself later on. If you ever need a Photoshop graphic done, drop me line and I will send you her details. I would Fiverr is ideal for designing website headers, graphics and logos, and for $5 you can't go far wrong!

If you want good content written, then a site like iWriter.com is a great place to start. Aim for over 750-1000 words if you can. And try to be as specific and clear in your requirements as possible – it will make a huge difference to the quality of work you receive back. Once submitted different writers will submit their work to you. The payment is held in Escrow, so you only pay for the work if you like it.

You can also check to see if they have copied any work you receive from elsewhere on the internet using a great site at Copyscape.com. This site allows you to do a limited number of free searches. However, it only costs 5 cents per search, so it's a good investment as you get lots of additional features using the Premium version. I bought 500 credits, which allows 500 searches, for $25. And I'm nowhere near using my allowance after nearly 2 years.

I will be talking more about the best ways to outsource your work on my website over the coming months.

Adwords

Adwords can work really well if you do it properly. It can get you instant results, rather than waiting for Google to index and get you up the rankings. However, it's also a great way to lose a lot of money if done badly. Adwords is a science in itself and needs to be done carefully. I've had great results using Adwords in certain niches, especially where competition is very high. Conversely, I have also lost a lot of money in other niches.

Facebook Marketing

Facebook Marketing is a big growth area and is becoming a serious challenge to Google Adwords. It is often cheaper than Adwords and it also allows for much more 'laser-targeted' marketing, so you can only show ads to say, women between 35 and 45. Again, great if done well, but it's simply throwing good money after bad if done wrong.

As with Adsense, your websites must be capable of converting users into customers first; it's no good getting 1,000 customers a day to your site if no-one ends up purchasing anything!

As they are such major topics in their own right I will be covering Adwords, Facebook and other forms of marketing on my own site, so keep checking in.

13. STATIC ELEMENTS

Panda/Penguin Alert

As part of the new algorithm changes, we all now know that Google wants to obliterate all the spammy, 'make a quick-buck and leave' sites. And, as we have discussed, the Googlebots gradually build a profile of the websites they crawl, picking up as many cues as they can as to gauge the trust level of each website. They want to see who the author is, whether the content is of a good quality, where else they are appearing on the internet, whether they have social accounts, how active they are, etc...

They are effectively asking themselves: 'how much can we trust this site? '. And as part of this checklist, they now want to be able to see certain static pages on your site, indicators that will tell them that you're a good and moral person and will be there for your audience and not some evil figure hiding in the shadows!

And Google now also wants your website to have the following pages in order to gain that extra level of trust:

- A Contact Us page;
- An About Us page;
- A Terms of Service or Terms & Conditions page;
- A Privacy Policy;
- A Disclaimer page (particularly if you're selling products or are an affiliate).

The contact page is important since it signals to Google that you're a real person with a real email address. Ideally, it also wants to see an address and a phone number on your site too. This won't be a problem for you if you're a business rather than an individual, so if this is the case then you really do need to include these. As an individual, I struggle with this and am not happy handing out all my personal details to the whole world. So I simply have my email address and a contact form on my sites.

The About Us page is always a good idea from both Google's and your user's perspectives as it engenders trust with both. In this section, just talk a little about yourself (and your team if you have one) in the form of a short Bio, what you're about, what your skills are, etc... It doesn't need to be overly long and is probably better if it isn't. If you don't have any links to your social profiles, then include these here too.

The Terms of Service page tells your visitors the kind of things you expect from them – that they shouldn't spam you or write abusive content on your site, that your content should not be copied, information on product warranties, etc.

Your Privacy Policy page tells your visitors the kind of things they should expect from you – that you won't share any information they give you to third parties, or

The Disclaimer page tells your visitors that your website is selling products or services and that you may be making money from them in some form.

These sections are not only for Google, but will serve to protect you in the eyes of the law, should any legal disputes arise (not that they ever should!).

It can be a real bind to write these pages, particularly the Terms of Service, Privacy Policy and Disclaimer pages. If you think you'll struggle with them, then don't fret: if you visit my website, you'll find examples of each in my Free Downloads section at:

http://onlyplacetogo.com/free-downloads

Just copy the content and paste them into your own pages. You simply need to amend the [insert your web address here] sections and insert your own website address.

Can I just ask that you try to personalize them as much as possible? Google is good at recognizing patterns and will see a 'footprint' and mark it down as duplicate content – make it your own as much as possible (you can even test to see how unique it is afterwards using Copyscape.com!).

Put links to each of these pages in your footer and then forget about them. Another task ticked off!

14. SUMMARY

I hope by now you're well on the way to having your site up and running.

You've:

- Registered your image on Gravatar;
- Signed up to Google Authorship;
- Linked Google+ to your Domain.
- You are getting into a routine of:
- Creating an Article;
- Posting it;
- Tweeting About it;
- Talking about it on Google+;
- Shouting about it on Facebook;
- Social Bookmarking it to at least 2 social bookmark sites;
- Talking about it on at least 2 Article Directory sites.
- Responded to the comments on your Blog (or even to your own comments to start with!).

And don't forget to follow others and join in the conversation by commenting on other relevant blogs.

Build up your comments gradually, and provide plenty of value. You'll be rewarded in spades.

As you progress, you can then start to give some thought thoughts to other forms of marketing, namely:

- YouTube Marketing;
- Facebook Marketing;
- Email marketing;
- Publishing your own book;
- Adwords.

Make sure you are following the FAIRER acronym to ensure your sites are:

- **F**unctional – users can navigate your site easily;
- **A**ctive – always up to date and filled with fresh content;
- **I**nteresting – attention grabbing articles with plenty of compelling content;
- **R**ich – full of great images, videos, charts, etc. to delight your audience;
- **E**njoyable – your site makes visitors want to come back for more;
- **R**elevant – you are providing exactly what the visitors are looking for.

Follow this pattern and you'll really start to see the fruits of your labors.

You'll need to get yourself organized so create a task list each day (preferably using pen and paper in a day-to-a-page A4 diary) and tick them off as you complete them.

Even the biggest projects can be broken down into lots of smaller tasks so it doesn't seem so overwhelming. It's incredibly motivating to tick-off your daily task and see your progress each day. Any you don't complete, just transfer them to the following day.

Give yourself allotted times for each task. And put them in order of priority, so you're not spending all day on unimportant tasks, like fine-tuning your header!

As you move forward and when your site starts to take off, you may also want to start outsourcing some of your work. Remember to be clear and concise in your requirements if you do.

To help you along the way, I'll even give you some help to get you started:

1. Send me an email along with your Website address, and I will add a link to it on my Website, under my 'Success Stories' section;
2. If you want, I'll also be happy to include a paragraph about your site or about you in this section too;
3. You can also send me your Facebook, Twitter and Google+ links and I'll be sure to Like You, Follow You and add you to my Inner Circle!

4. If you want to do any guest posting on my site, onlyplacetogo.com, let me know and I'll be happy to post them too.

5. An invitation to join my private 'How to Rank in Google' Facebook group. As one of my valued readers, you'll be one of my VIPs! Just drop me a line and I'll send you an invitation, or visit:

   https://www.facebook.com/groups/436859713068601

   and click on 'Join Group' icon.

6. Finally, please feel free to drop me a line at james@onlyplacetogo.com with any questions, views, your success stories or your ideas and I'll do my best to respond.

These backlinks are not for Google, they're for your visitors, so promote yourself! I put this website together for YOU, so please make use of it – we're in this together!

All I ask in return is that you give me an honest review of my book on Amazon. I do hope you enjoyed it and that it's given you plenty of food for thought as well as inspiration to get out there and make a real success of yourself and your site.

So make a commitment today to follow all the strategies in this book and I promise you will see amazing results. Do it half-heartedly and you'll be disappointed. Remember, you only need to be slightly better than the next guy to be a fantastic success!

So just keep that forward motion going. And joining my Facebook group will help to keep that fire burning and those light bulb moments flashing!

You've made it this far and I've got every confidence in you!

I wish you the very best of luck in all your endeavors.

Keep in Touch,

James

APPENDIX OF USEFUL SITES

Below are all the websites and tools I use. I won't say they're necessarily the best, but they've all served me well over the years:

Platform of choice

WordPress (wordpress.org) – Hands down, the easiest way to get a website up and running, with great SEO tools.

Outsourcing sites

Fiverr (fiverr.com) – One of my favorites. Great for designing, logos, header graphics or on-page images, Kindle book covers, even transcription services. And it's cheap!

iWriter (iwriter.com) – a relatively inexpensive way to get pretty good articles written for your site.

Elance (elance.com) – another great place to get articles written, but they also do a whole variety of other tasks such as web design and programming.

oDesk (oDesk.com) – Very similar to Elance.

Words into Profits (wordsintoprofits.com) – a great transcription service that will transcribe your spoken word.

Hosting Account

Hostgator (hostgator.com) – the only hoster I use, inexpensive and allows for unlimited domains for a very reasonable monthly fee.

SEO Tools

Traffic Travis (traffictravis.com) – free, invaluable SEO software for checking out your competition.

SEOQuake (seoquake.com) – a great FireFox plug-in that gives a lot of in-depth information about any website.

Search Status (quirk.biz/searchstatus) – another useful FireFox plug-in.

Stock Photography Sites

iStockPhoto (istockphoto.com)

Shutterstock (shutterstock.com)

Stock Exchange (sxc.hu)

Social Sites

Google+ (plus.google.com)

Twitter (twitter.com)

Facebook (facebook.com)

Graphics software

Photoshop (adobe.com/uk/products/photoshop.html) - Expensive, but invaluable if you want to create stunning vector-based artwork.

Fireworks (adobe.com/uk/products/fireworks.html) – My old reliable graphics software. I use an older version which still serves me well.

Paint.net – Free paint software that's easy to use. Great for doing simple header graphics.

Social Bookmarking sites

Digg (Digg.com)
Reddit (Reddit.com)
Delicious (Delicious.com)
Folkd (Folkd.com)
Article directories
WordPress.com
Tumblr.com
Hubpages.com

Livestrong.com
Ask.com
Ezinearticles.com
Livejournal.com
Ezinearticles.com

Dictation / Video Editing

Windows 7 Speech Recognition – Free software bundled with Windows 7 that works surprisingly well.
Camtasia Studio (www.techsmith.com/camtasia.html) – Not cheap, but excellent professional video editing software.
Camstudio (camstudio.org) – a free alternative to Camtasia, that's great for making screen-capture videos.
Audacity (audacity.sourceforge.net) – free recording software to record your articles to a sound file.

Buying/Selling domain sites

Freshdrop (freshdrop.net) – a domain auction site, where you can pick up high PR domains very cheaply, if you're patient.
Flippa (flippa.com)

Other sites

Gravatar (gravatar.com) – a must to create an expert presence on the web.
YouTube (youtube.com) – for video marketing your site.
Amazon Publishing (kdp.amazon.com) – the only place to go to self-publish your books.
Pagemodo (pagemodo.com) – for creating nice looking Facebook headers.
Aweber (aweber.com) – a great, if a little expensive email marketing campaign tool. Use when your sites are established.
Copyscape (copyscape.com) – a tool for checking for plagiarism.
Affilorama (affilorama.com) – the site where I really began to understand the power of affiliate marketing.